Cells Are Us

by Dr. Fran Balkwill
illustrated by Mic Rolph

Carolrhoda Books, Inc./Minneapolis

This edition first published 1993 by Carolrhoda Books, Inc.

Carolrhoda Books, Inc.
A Division of the Lerner Publishing Group
241 First Avenue North
Minneapolis, MN 55401 U.S.A.
Website address: www.lernerbooks.com

Library of Congress Cataloging-in-Publication Data

Balkwill, Francis R.
    Cells are us / by Fran Balkwill; illustrated by Mic Rolph.
        p.   cm.
    Originally published: London: W. Collins, 1990.
    Summary: Explains the functions of the cells in the human body.
    ISBN 0-87614-762-7
    1.Cells — Juvenile literature. 2. Cell differentiation — Juvenile literature.
    [1. Cells.] I. Rolph, Mic, ill. 11. Title.
    QH582.5.B35   1993
    611'.0181—dc20   92-8867

Printed in Hong Kong
Bound in the United States of America

7 8 9 10 11- OS - 06 05 04 03 02

Once upon a time, before you were born, two cells collided, one bigger than the other. The bigger cell (the egg) and the smaller cell (the sperm) became one very special cell...

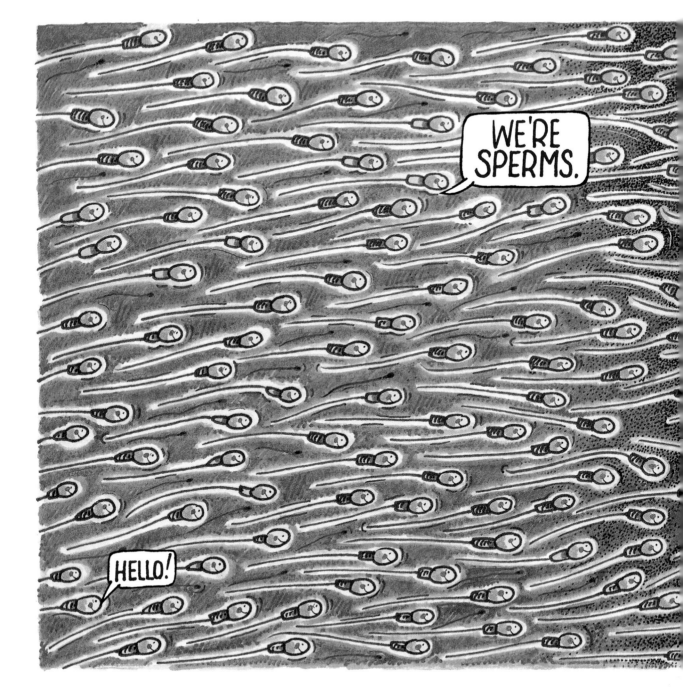

YOU WERE
MADE

Every living creature on earth, from ants to zebras, from worms to whales, began life just as you did – as a single tiny cell.

But what are cells?

Cells are the "building blocks" of life. Your body is made of millions and millions of them. Each one is so tiny you can't even see it with a magnifying glass. You need to use a microscope.

When you look at cells under a microscope using a very powerful lens, you can clearly see hundreds of them. With the most powerful lens, you can see a single cell close up.

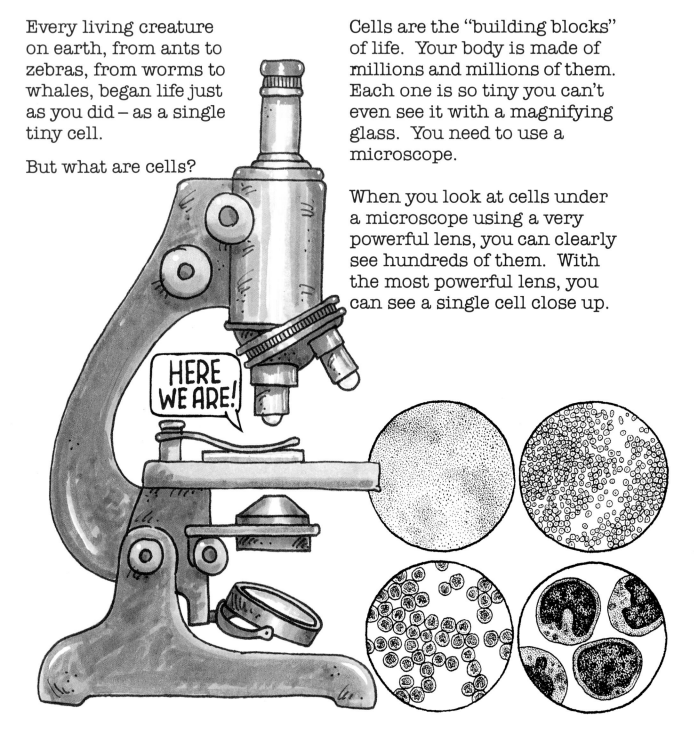

But how did you grow from just one cell?

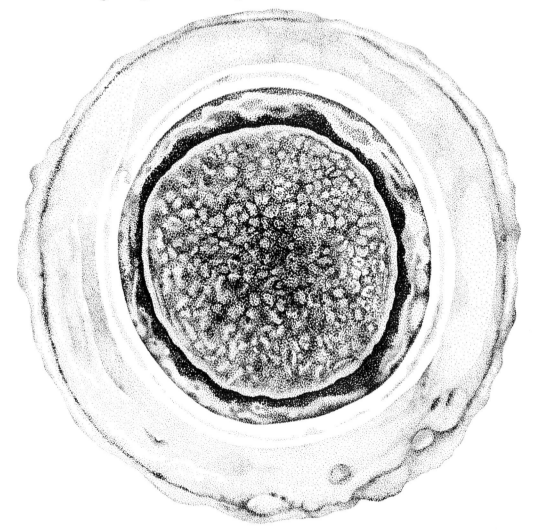

That first cell had all the information and instructions to make you the way you are now. This information was all in a secret code in the middle of the cell. This code is called DNA. It is a very long list of instructions that gives each cell in your body its own shape and function.

That first cell grew a little, and soon wiggly parts called
chromosomes (KROH-muh-sohmz) could be seen inside the cell.

Half of the chromosomes came from the egg cell, and half
from the sperm cell, and each chromosome contained two
copies of that secret code, the plans for making you.

The first cell then divided into two separate cells, using a process called cell division. This is how it happened.

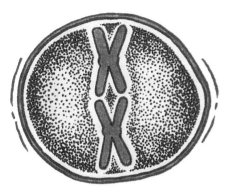

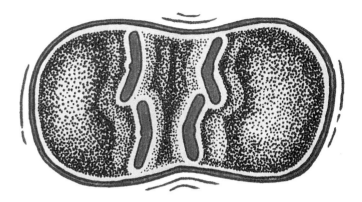

First the chromosomes lined up in the center of the cell.

Then each chromosome split into two identical pairs.

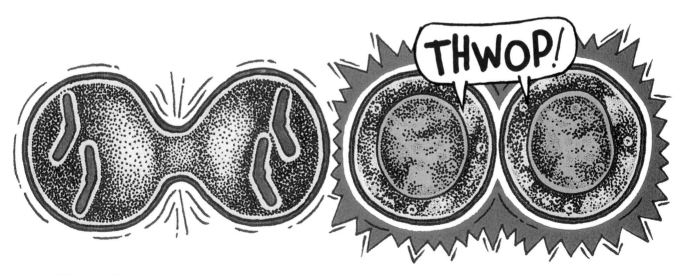

THWOP!

Next the pairs of chromosomes moved to opposite ends of the cell, and...

TA-DA!!! Two cells, which both had all the information and instructions to make you...and then...

Those 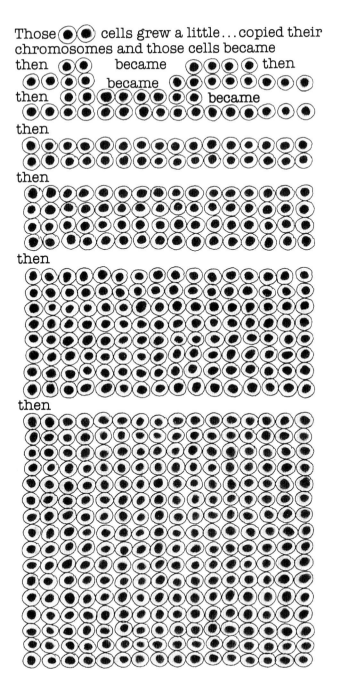 cells grew a little... copied their chromosomes and those cells became

then became then

became

then became

then

then

then

then

then

Very soon there were

MILLIONS

Millions of cells that now began to
look different from each other...

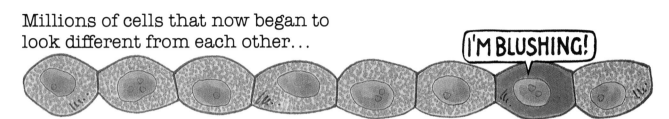

Some became the cells that make your skin.

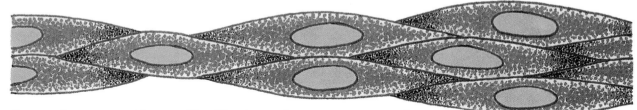

Some became the cells that make your muscles.

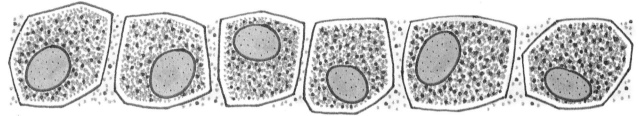

Some became the bone cells that make your skeleton.

Some became the blood cells that carry oxygen around your body.

Some became the nerve cells that carry messages from your brain.
And so on. There are over 200 different cell types in your body.

11

But your cells didn't really grow in straight lines. They grew in a ball shape like this.

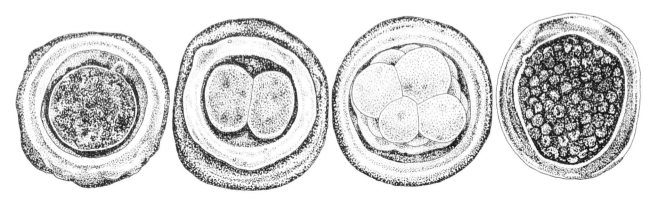

Still doesn't look much like *you*, does it?

As your cells began to make more and more cells, the ball of cells began to change shape.

Soon you had a head, tiny arms, legs, and a tail!

Yes, you once had a tail.

At this stage, it looks as if you were going to turn into a fish.

But you didn't, did you?

12

Your cells kept growing and dividing, so that after about 40 weeks (9 months), that very first cell had divided into millions and millions of cells doing all kinds of different, difficult, and amazing jobs, so that when you were born you could

Of course, you didn't stop there. You kept on growing because your cells kept on dividing, and you haven't stopped growing yet.

So now it's time to be introduced to some of your cells and find out about the jobs they do. But remember…cells are so tiny that you could fit a hundred or more on the period at the end of this sentence.

If one of your cells was really this size  you'd be as tall as the Empire State Building.

½ in.

TOOT!

15

Let's start with the outside of your body. Skin cells have the important job of protecting your insides and outsides from extremes of cold and heat, from sharp or sticky objects, from wind, rain, and dirt. They make a layer about ten living cells deep, and they keep it that way by replacing themselves regularly.

Some cells move up through the layers as they get older, becoming tougher and scalier. When they die, they float off into the air to form dust.

Some parts of your skin need to be tougher than others, so the layer of dead cells gets thicker to protect you. The skin on your heel, for example, is tougher than the skin on your face.

Did you know that millions of skin cells float off your body every day? Give your leg a quick scratch. There, you just got rid of a few hundred thousand skin cells.

Skin cells also give your body its color. No matter who you are...

...everybody's skin cells are exactly the same, except that they make different amounts of special substances called **melanin** (MEL-uh-nin) and **carotene** (KAR-oh-teen). If your skin is pale and you go out in the sun, your cells make more melanin. That's how you get a tan. But be careful — too much sun can make you sick.

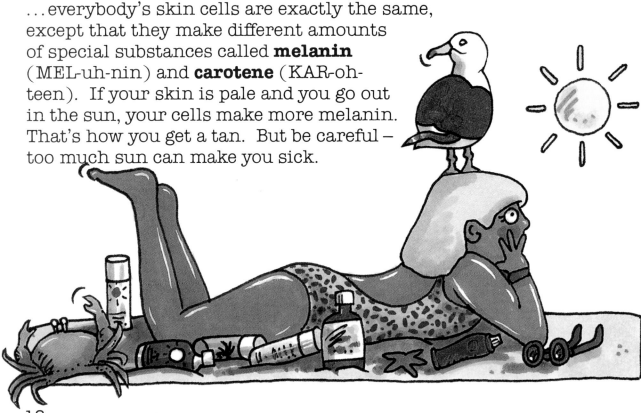

Now we'll go inside your body. All your cells need food to help them grow and divide. Blood carries cell food around your body, into every nook and cranny.

Blood flows from your heart through big tubes called **arteries.**
Arteries connect to much smaller tubes called **capillaries**
(KAP-uh-ler-eez), which in turn connect to big tubes called
veins (VAYNZ). Veins carry blood back to your heart.

Blood is liquid, isn't it?
But what does that liquid contain?
Yes, you guessed it (well, if you haven't, just pretend).
That's right. Cells.

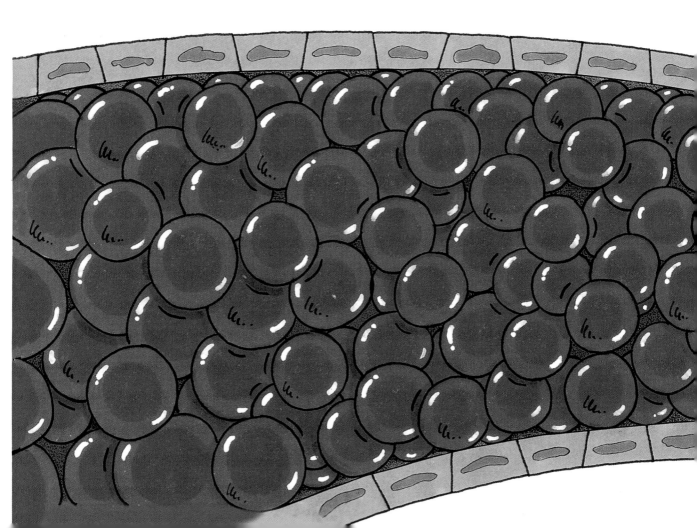

Blood is always red because it contains zillions of red blood cells.

Did you know that your body has to make about one hundred fifty million blood cells every minute of your life to replace the ones that die?

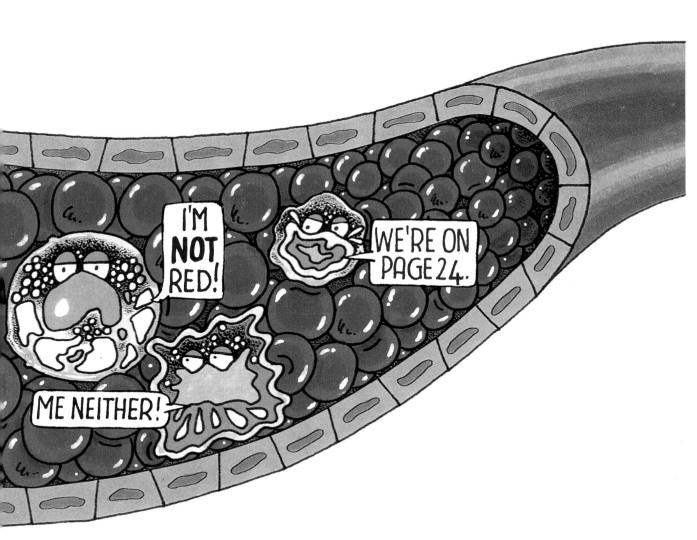

The red cells in your blood have an important job to do. They carry a gas called **oxygen** (AHK-sih-jen) around your body. Without oxygen, all your cells would die. The air that you breathe into your lungs contains oxygen.

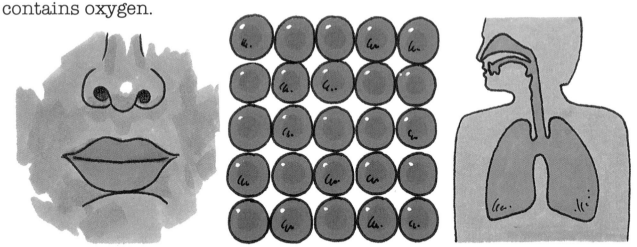

Take a deep breath! **Hemoglobin** (HEE-muh-gloh-bin), a special substance in red blood cells, gets oxygen from your lung cells,

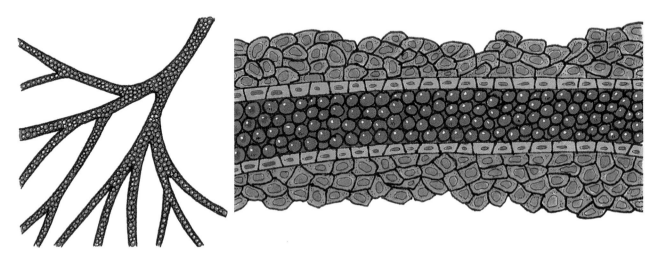

takes it through your bloodstream, and releases it to cells that need it. When each breath of oxygen has been used up,

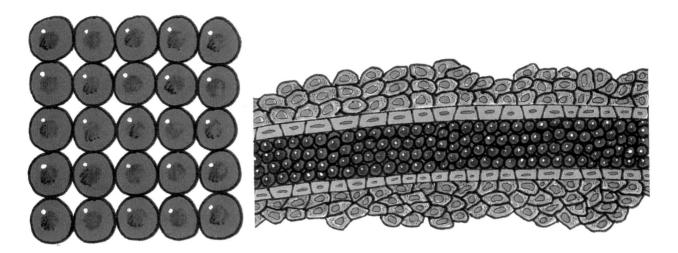

another gas (not such a nice one), called carbon dioxide, remains. The air that you breathe out contains carbon dioxide.

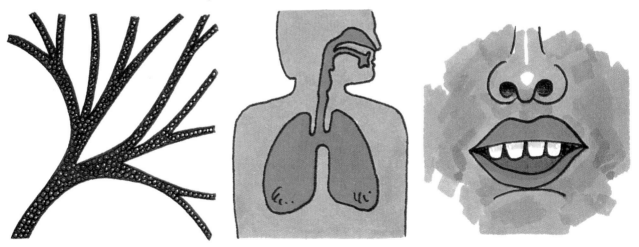

Red blood cells carry the carbon dioxide back through the capillaries and veins to the lungs. Now breathe out!

You have some other very special blood cells, **neutrophils** (NOO-tro-filz), **macrophages** (MAK-ruh-fay-jez), and **lymphocytes** (LIM-fuh-sytz).

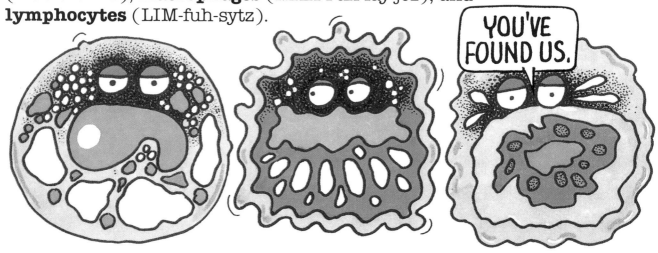

These cells aren't red, they are white. They are your defender cells.

Their job is to constantly patrol the bloodstream, fighting off all the nasty things such as viruses and bacteria that make you ill.

If white blood cells don't destroy the bad germs right away, they send for reinforcements, and millions more white cells join in.

So when you've got measles, or wheezles, or sneezles, remember your white blood cells are working to make you better.

Do you imagine that cells are sort of squishy things? Then what do you suppose your bones are made of? Surely bones aren't made of cells. Yes, surprisingly, they are.

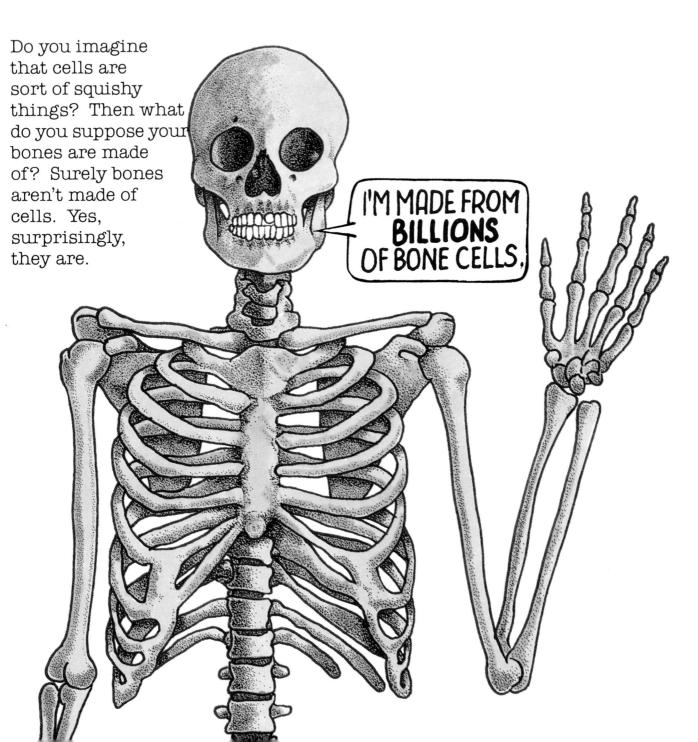

I'M MADE FROM **BILLIONS** OF BONE CELLS,

But how do bone cells make your skeleton? Well, each bone cell is like a factory, churning out really tough stuff that surrounds the cells and hardens.

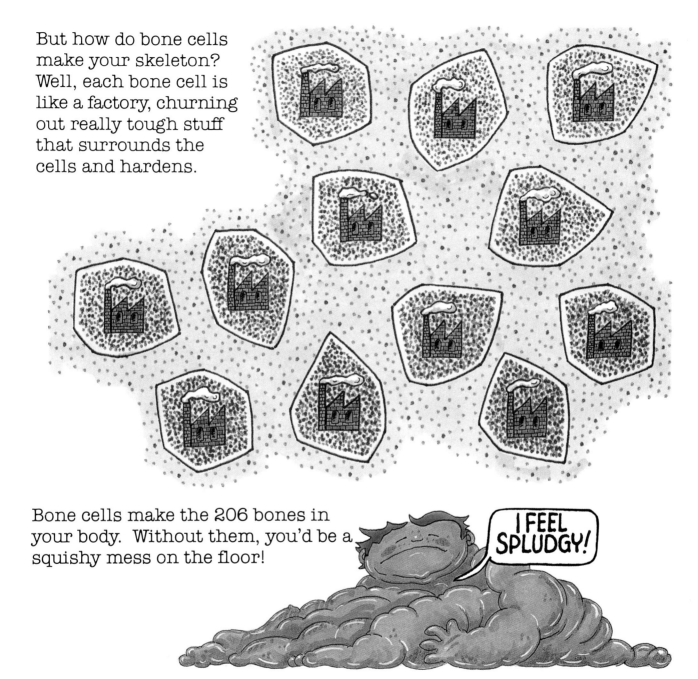

Bone cells make the 206 bones in your body. Without them, you'd be a squishy mess on the floor!

I FEEL SPLUDGY!

Muscle cells are long, thin, S-T-R-E-T-C-H-Y cells that make every part of your body move.

Each cell contains tiny strands of stretchy substances called **actin** and **myosin** that can make the cell change size and shape.

Muscle cells are tightly joined together so that they all change shape at the same time.

As a muscle contracts (gets shorter) or expands (gets bigger),

Nerve cells are excitable cells that send messages around your body by tiny electrical impulses. These messages travel along threadlike parts of nerve cells called **axons.**

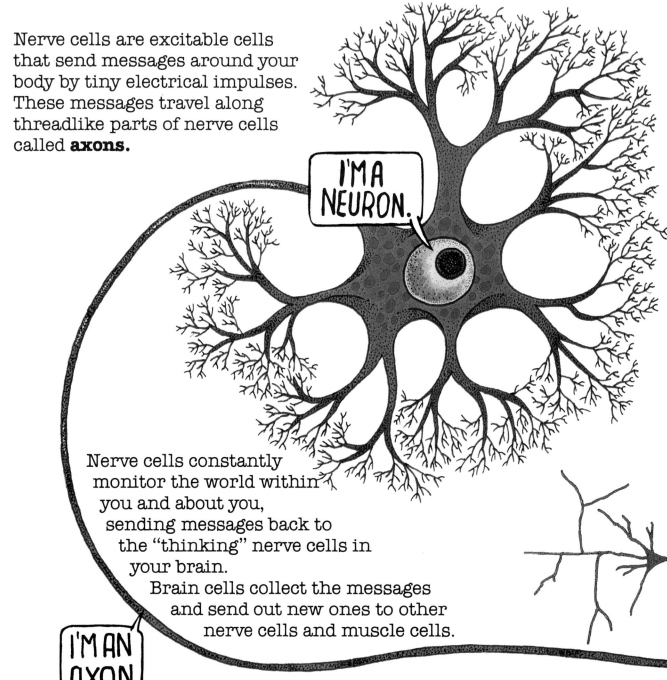

Nerve cells constantly monitor the world within you and about you, sending messages back to the "thinking" nerve cells in your brain.
Brain cells collect the messages and send out new ones to other nerve cells and muscle cells.

Some nerve cells in your brain keep parts of your body working without your thinking about it, even when you are fast asleep. You don't have to remember to breathe or make your heart beat, do you?

Nerve cells come in some surprising shapes and sizes. One type of nerve cell that controls your leg and arm muscles is the same width as other cells in your body but can be up to 40 inches (1 meter) long!

There are, of course, many other cells in your body, including cells that work your stomach, lungs, liver, and kidneys, and cells that make your teeth, nails, and hair. Scientists all over the world have learned a lot about your amazing body – but they still don't know the whole story.

As scientists learn more about cells, they should be able to find new cures for diseases such as cancer and AIDS.

The exciting challenge for future scientists (maybe you?) is to understand completely how all those millions of cells work together in harmony to make you grow and keep you healthy, and how they developed in such a precise and detailed pattern – all from that first tiny cell that was you.

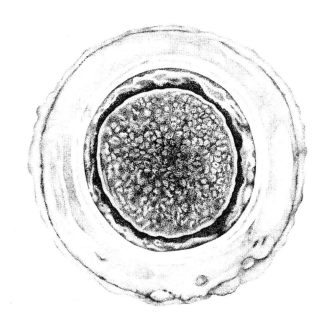